From ALCOHOLISM to AWESOME!

SHANNON AND AURELIE REEVE

Copyright © 2016 by Shannon and Aurelie Reeve

From Alcoholism to Awesome!
by Shannon and Aurelie Reeve

Printed in the United States of America.

ISBN 9781498457705

All rights reserved solely by the author. The author guarantees all contents are original and do not infringe upon the legal rights of any other person or work. No part of this book may be reproduced in any form without the permission of the author. The views expressed in this book are not necessarily those of the publisher.

Unless otherwise indicated, Scripture quotations taken from the Holy Bible, New Living Translation. Copyright ©1996, 2004, 2007 by Tyndale House Foundation. Used by permission of Tyndale House Publishers, Inc.

www.xulonpress.com

Dedication

*Our story is dedicated to our Lord Jesus Christ,
and to our children and grandchildren.*

TABLE OF CONTENTS

Acknowledgments vii
Introduction: Last Chance. ix

Chapter 1:   The Life and Times of Shannon Reeve 13
Chapter 2:   Marriage and Family 19
Chapter 3:   Hitting Bottom. 27
Chapter 4:   Into His Waiting Arms 35
Chapter 5:   God's Plan for My Life 43
Chapter 6:   Aurelie's Walk with Jesus 53
Chapter 7:   Our Daughters' Stories 68

Conclusion: Walking with the Lord 79

ACKNOWLEDGMENTS

We are so thankful to God for Pastor Cameron and his wife, Marge, for their huge influence on us in the church where we gave our lives to the Lord.

We thank our children for sharing their hearts with us as we wrote this book.

We are thankful to Xulon Press and the editorial team of Dr. Larry Keefauver and Pam McLaughlin for their assistance in writing and publishing our book.

We are so grateful to our church family for never giving up on us and staying so supportive of us.

Introduction

LAST CHANCE

A brand new semi-truck rolled, the driver was unscathed, but the owner of the truck had been sleeping in the sleeper and was thrown from the bunks. Twenty minutes earlier, they had switched drivers. Now Shannon Reeve was laying in Kenora Hospital with fractured bones in his spine, 1700 kilometers from home and his wife Aurelie! Life as he knew it had forever changed. His life-long dream and his brand new semi-truck were in rough shape. There was a 130K loan that would soon be screaming for payments. There were fuel bills, insurance bills, tires, and welding that needed to be done to repair the truck, and Shannon couldn't work until his truck was fixed. Ontario has a no fault law meaning there was no insurance money to cover the heavy burden!

Aurelie was working at the bank, but not making enough to cover even their daily living expenses, never mind a $3,000 a month truck payment. To go bankrupt was not an option because she would lose her job if we did. Bill collectors were understanding at first while waiting for the truck to be repaired so Shannon could get back to work again. The accident was in August of 1999, he got his truck back the end of November and was back to work in December. Shannon made it until the first of the year when they received more bad news.

Shannon had been in constant pain and had gone back to the doctors for a check-up. It was then they discovered his back was broken in two places. Workers Compensation Board became Shannon's only source of income at under $1,000 a month, which combined with Aurelie's wage was barely enough to keep their heads above water personally, never mind the business! Months of postponing collectors and the leasing company went by. In February, they had to give the truck back to the leasing company. Day by day things got progressively harder as the bills piled up even higher. They did not want to answer the phone knowing it would be somebody demanding money.

"One day Shannon came to see me at work," Aurelie shares. "When he left I knew something was very wrong, so I called my brother and asked him to please go out and be with my husband. I was afraid he was going to take his own life. When my brother arrived, Shannon was sitting in the vehicle in the garage with the engine running. The two of them went in the house with a bottle of rum. Drowning his sorrows in alcohol always seemed to be the answer anytime Shannon was upset with life."

"Going back a few years I tried to quit drinking through AA because I did not like who I had become," Shannon shares with a sad shake of his head. "Aurelie and I would go and play cards with my sponsor. I almost got a year pin for being sober, though I never was for more than a day or so at a time."

"Though I wanted to be a better husband and a father, for the next six years I battled with alcohol," Shannon remembers. "I was working for a construction company at the time and I would just tell my boss to get me jobs out of town. I would be okay for a couple of days. Thursday night was party night, then Friday morning I would get all sobered up so I could go home."

Then in September of 2001, Aurelie's grandmother passed away. We went to the funeral on Saturday and then some of us went to our place to drink because that is what we did after a funeral. The next morning, Aurelie's sister and her husband who were up from B.C. phoned and asked Aurelie if she wanted to go to church. After you bury someone you think about life after death and what that looks like, so Aurelie said yes.

"When she asked me if I wanted to go; I said absolutely not!" Shannon admits.

Then Aurelie started bugging the kids to get ready to go with her.

"I started swearing at her to make sure she understood that I meant no," Shannon remembers. "I don't know why, but all of a sudden I got up and started getting ready to go, telling them I had decided to drive them there and drop them off."

When they got to the church, instead of dropping them off, Shannon declared, "Ah, what the heck, I'll come in with you, but we're sitting right at the back, and when that guy says *Amen* we're out of here."

It was a Pentecostal church and the worship was upbeat. After the service, the pastor had an altar call. Then Shannon got the surprise of his life.

"At that moment, I saw Jesus standing at the end of our pew," Shannon remembers. "He held His hand out and I knew that was my moment—that was my chance to make a choice. I knew that I either had to go up and do something about my life or I was going to die. I knew this was my **last chance** to do something about it."

Chapter 1

THE LIFE AND TIMES OF SHANNON REEVE

I was born and raised in Edmonton. I had an older sister and a younger brother. My dad was an abusive alcoholic. He would come home drunk just about every night, then he and my mom would fight. He would hit her and punch her. Around the age of ten, I started sticking up for my mom and then I started getting slapped around, too. He was a mean drunk and slept around and cheated on mom, as well. Finally, when I was twelve, my mom left us. I missed my mom. I loved her more than anything in the world. It took a couple of months but then the moment that I had a chance, I ran away from home to be with her. When I found her at my grandfather's house, my mom and my grandfather took me back to the house to get my stuff so that I could stay with my Mom. She agreed I should not have to stay with my dad.

Though I do not remember all the details, we ended up in family court. The judge said I was old enough to pick who I wanted to live with. Of course, I said I wanted to stay with my mom. After that, we went to my dad's house to get the rest of my stuff. We drove away and I never looked back. I did not talk to or have anything to do with my dad for quite a few years after that.

My mom and I started a new life together. I went back to school for a while. I had been a straight A student in spite of the situation at home. In fact, I skipped third grade and went from second to fourth grade. Mom and I lived together for quite a while. I had a great deal of trouble adjusting especially after Mom met another man and we moved in with him. My grades started slipping, and I started getting in lots of trouble in school. I ended up getting expelled.

Frustrated and feeling there was nothing they could do to help me, Mom and George, my step-father, said that the only thing that would work for me was to go back and be with my dad. So, I went back and lived with him. My dad was remarried by then and my step-mother wasn't that fond of me or my siblings. She had children of her own and they were her family while my sister and brother and I were kind of just there. We never felt like it was our home. My dad only hit my step-mother once. She told him if he ever did it again she would walk away. He still drank a lot, though.

> **Like many children who grow up in an alcoholic or abusive home, I told myself I would never be like my father, but that is just what I did.**

This is when I really started getting into alcohol and drugs. Any opportunity I had, I drank and got high because then I didn't feel anything or care about anything. They put me in a Catholic school, but I kept getting into trouble there as well. It didn't work out to live with my dad, so I ended up going back to live with my mom and my step-dad. Then we moved to Peace River into an apartment above a clothing store owned by my step-dad's sister.

They enrolled me in a new school and I entered the eighth grade. I was in social studies class one day and we were watching a movie. The teacher, who was also the vice principal, left the room. One of the kids in my class and I were messing around. Suddenly, he'd had enough and got up, getting mouthy with me. Always on the verge of uncontrolled anger, I threw him down on the ground and quickly climbed up on top of my desk. As I jumped up in the air, I turned and saw the teacher opening the door. It was too late to stop; I was already in the air and landed on top of him. Of course, I got kicked out of class and sat in the hallway for the rest of the period. When she took me down to her office to talk to me after class, I was my regular disrespectful self, even threatening her and telling her she couldn't kick me out of school because I would get her fired. I was just an idiot and she kicked me out of school.

That night I had to tell my mom and step-dad I had been expelled from school again, and my step-dad looked at me and said, "If I get you back in school this time are you going to stay?"

Shaking my head, I said, "Probably not."

He simply said, "Fine, tomorrow go look for a job."

I thought, *Sweet, I'll just sit around and kind of look for a job. Nothing really says I have to, but I don't ever have to go back to school.* I was fourteen years old and thinking my chances of getting a job were slim to none, anyway. However, the very next day my mom came home from work and told me the husband of a lady she was working with said the gas company was hiring, and she got me a job. The job was in Fairview, which was over an hour away. Well, my heart just fell into my stomach, but I didn't say anything or show any emotion. That night they packed my bags, drove me to Fairview, and booked me in a hotel room for the next two weeks. Then they showed me where I had to be in the morning for work, gave me a little bit of money, said *goodbye*, and drove away.

Here I was, this mean fourteen-year-old-kid, standing there in that hotel room, watching them drive away, and I bawled like a two-year-old baby. I was so scared, but there was no way I was going to tell anybody. I certainly wasn't going back to school. The next morning, I got up and I went to work. I worked there for quite a few years, and worked my way up the ranks. However, by the time I was sixteen, I was a full blown alcoholic, drinking every day.

With a steady paycheck, I found my own place and rented a room in a renovated house that had a bed, a fridge, a table, and a hot plate. I shared that five-room house where we all shared the bathroom. There were two older guys also living there. This one guy in particular who must have been in his seventies, took me under his wing and was just like my grandfather. He was good to me and looked after me. If he didn't hear me getting up in the morning and showering, he'd come over and knock on my door. He knew I was probably hung over, but he would tell me I better get up and get going to work. With no car and no driver's license, I hitch hiked back and forth to work for a couple of years.

When I was a little over sixteen, I left that job and went back to Grimshaw where my mom and step-dad lived, and started working for him building houses. I would build houses as long as the weather permitted, and then in the winter when construction was slow, I'd drive truck. That's what brought me to Barrhead. I ended up drunk, got in a fight, and was pushed down a flight of stairs which broke my collar bone. Now I could no longer work construction. I remembered my Uncle lived in Barrhead and owned a New Holland Dealership. So, I phoned him and asked him if he could use anybody to haul the equipment around. Driving truck would not further damage my shoulder. He agreed to hire me and let me live in his basement. That's what I did for about the next two years, but I still went out drinking all the time.

Digging Deeper

Go back to your family of origin, think about your growing up years, and ask yourself these questions:
- *What kind of relationship did my parents have with each other?*
- *What kind of relationship did I have with my father?*
- *What kind of relationship did I have with my mother?*
- *Did they tell me that they loved me?*
- *If not, did I feel loved?*
- *What was my relationship with my siblings?*

As you grew and entered your teenage years, think about the influence these relationships had on your decision making process.
- *Did you vow to not be like one of your parents or another family member?*
- *What choices or decisions did you make as a teenager or young adult that you now think were negatively influenced by your childhood relationships?*
- *What choices or decisions were influenced positively by those relationships?*

Read these scriptures to discover God's method of helping you with the decision making process.

Psalm 119:105

Proverbs 3:5-6

Isaiah 48:17

Pray and ask God to help you with any decisions you find you need to make today. Thank Him for being available to help you and guide you as you seek Him first each day.

Chapter 2

MARRIAGE AND FAMILY

Though I [Shannon] was very close with my mom, I never had much regard for women in general. I wanted what I wanted, when I wanted it, and I did whatever I had to do to get it. I never raped for it, but I would sweet talk, I would lie, I would pay for it, I would do anything I had to do. I didn't care. Once I was done getting what I wanted, I'd just move on and had no feelings whatsoever for anything or anyone but myself.

Nonetheless, when I met Aurelie I treated her the same way I had every woman in my past, but for some crazy reason she stuck around. Aurelie was sixteen and I was nineteen when we met. We went out a few times and she kept hunting me down if I didn't show up when I was supposed to. We continued to date, and I ended up getting her pregnant; so, she quit school. We got married, moved back to where my mom and step-dad lived, and I went back to work for my step-dad building houses. I was still majorly into alcohol, but I slowed down immensely on the drugs when my daughter, Stefanie, was born. I looked at her in the hospital, and I made her a promise that I would stop doing drugs. Trying to keep my promise, I just turned to alcohol even more.

We had good times, but we had a whole lot of bad times, too. I couldn't get my act together, I was drunk all the time. Verbally abusive, I was a mean drunk just like my dad. Once in a while I was physically abusive, though I never beat Aurelie. I would grab her and throw her up against the wall, threaten her, and call her names.

Once I was so full of pride and acting like such an idiot, I threw a drink in her face and said, "I'm going to the top and if you don't want to come with me that's your problem."

I was arrogant and not going anywhere but down. Aurelie came right back at me and said she was going to leave me if I didn't go to AA. Packing a bag, I left for a day or two, but we never did stay apart for very long. I think God kept us together. However, I did finally agree to go to AA; I almost got a one-year sober pin. All I did, though, when I was in AA was to ask my boss to send me out of town so I could drink and nobody would know it. My boss was an alcoholic as well, so he would send me out of town all the time to help me hide my drinking from my wife and my sponsor.

Though I drank all week, Thursday night would be my big party night. Friday I'd come home and wouldn't drink all weekend. Then I would go to AA, go to my sponsor's house to play cards, and brag about how good it was not to be a drunk. Monday, it was back to work and back to getting drunk every night. That lasted about a year until everybody caught on to what was going on. Then we moved because I got caught, no one understood me, and it was never my fault.

We would always move away from my problems, but I was still there and so were my issues.

It was always good when we moved to somewhere new. It was like a new beginning and another chance to do it right this time. However, once I started working and meeting people, then I could start going to the bar with them, and drinking at work with them. I would fall right back into the same old routine. Sometimes, though, it wasn't because we were running from alcohol related problems. Some of it was because we were running to a job because we had run out of work. I would have to find a job somewhere else. One of our moves came because I began driving a log truck for my father-in-law. I kept logging and things were good, so I bought my own truck and even hired a second driver to work with me. Lots of things went good, but I was still drinking and partying all the time. Alcohol is a costly habit, and though I was making good money, we seemed to be broke all the time. This caused us to be fighting all the time.

God's Hand on My Life

Then in August of 1999, as I shared earlier, I was sleeping in the bunk of my truck when my driver rolled the truck. It threw me out of the bunk and did eighty thousand dollars' worth of damage to my truck. I ended up in the hospital 1700 kilometers from home, and no way to get back. Aurelie and some really good friends of ours drove all the way there to pick me up and take me out of the hospital. It took us three days to get home because I couldn't travel very long at one time due to the intense pain in my back. It wasn't until I got home and went to the doctor there that he sent me to the specialist in Edmonton. They realized I had a broken back in three places and couldn't figure out what I was doing walking around.

Of course, all of this just gave me more reason to drink. There were days I might be drunk by 11:00 a.m. in the morning. Sometimes I would come home after an early morning binge and fall out of the truck because

I couldn't even stand up I was so drunk. When Aurelie talks about this time in our lives, she says she can't believe I didn't die of alcohol poisoning or drive my pick-up truck off the road I drank so much.

Too many times to count, I would have the gas pedal to the floor and come up to the corner and think it was my street. Then I'd jam on the breaks so hard my truck would go sideways. Once I realized it wasn't my corner, I'd give it the gas again and speed to the next corner and do it again. Now when I drive that same highway and all the embankments I could have gone over, I just know God had His hand in it.

It's unbelievable how many times God had to keep me alive.

Through my stint with alcoholism, I had six arrests for driving while impaired, though I probably should have had at least twenty-six! I would even drink and drive after I had lost my driver's license for driving while impaired. Aurelie knew when I was out drinking that if I drank, I would drive the truck so she did her best to try and stop me. One memory I have of her attempt to protect me in my drunken state is that she flattened all four tires and took the battery cables off my truck. I walked out in the parking lot of the bar and went to start my truck. When it wouldn't start, I laughed as I thought, she thinks I'm stupid. I lift up the hood, put that battery cable back on, and started driving down the road. Then I realized I was driving on four flat tires. Yes, I guess I'm that stupid. I didn't even know I had four flat tires.

After the accident with the big truck that broke my back, things just started going downhill fast. Bills started coming in, truck payments were still due, but now I had no truck to use for work. The insurance company wanted to fix it and not write it off, so I had to wait for it to be repaired. As it turned out, I wouldn't have been able to drive it anyways; I was in too much pain. I still had all the bills and the little money Workers' Compensation paid me didn't even come close to meeting our needs.

Aurelie had a job at a bank so bankruptcy wasn't even on the table because she would have lost her job if we'd filed for it. We just fought, lied, cheated, and struggled through it. I contemplated suicide several times, but it seemed every time I came home with that in mind, our neighbor's little piglets would break out and be all over the road. I would just start laughing and help my neighbor get them back in his barn. I guess that was just another one of God's ways of stopping me from doing something foolish.

Then one day, I went to town to where Aurelie was working. After talking to her for a little while about trivial things, I kissed her and said goodbye, and walked out of the bank. On my way home, I just started of thinking of suicide again. Somehow, Aurelie knew. I think God told her. So, she phoned her brother and told him to get right out and see what was going on with me because she thought I was planning to commit suicide. For some reason that day, there were no piglets in the road. I drove into our garage and closed the garage door behind me. Then I left my truck running and just sat back in the driver's seat waiting to go asleep forever.

It wasn't more than a few minutes later I heard a truck pull in the yard. Of course, I shut everything off, went in the house and pretended like I just got home and nothing was going on. Sure enough it was Aurelie's brother, so we sat there and got drunk. He never said Aurelie had sent him, but he stayed with me nonetheless.

Looking back, I know God was doing all of this to keep me safe until I came to my senses and realized He was the answer.

Digging Deeper

Running away from our problems is never the way to solve them. So many times we think changing jobs, changing locations, and even changing marriage partners will solve all our problems. Somehow, though, that never seems to work the way we think it will. That is because, if we would just be honest with ourselves, the real problem is deep within us. The reason changing positions, locations, or partners doesn't work is because we bring the issues with us to these new positions, new locations, and new relationships.

It is time to be really honest with yourself. Ask yourself these questions and give a straight and honest answer. The only way you are going to get at the root of the problem is by being truthful with yourself and with God.

Why did you leave your last job?
Who did you blame?
Why did you leave your last home or apartment?
What or who did you blame?
Why did you leave that last relationship?
Whose fault was the break-up?

Now it is time to reevaluate the situations. Ask these questions again from a different perspective:

What did I do to make that job situation a problem?
What should I have done instead of leaving?
What did I do to cause the unrest in my last neighborhood or apartment complex?
What should I have done to diffuse the situation?
What did I do to jeopardize that relationship?

What should I do to reconcile or restore an amicable relationship with that person?

Read these scriptures to discover what God says about relationships with Him and with others.
Job 42:10
Psalm 1:1-2
Colossians 3:8-10

Pray and ask God to help you with any relationships in your life that are strained or in trouble. Be willing to do whatever it takes to restore your relationship with God and with others. Stop blaming others and begin to take responsibility for your own decisions and choices.

Chapter 3
HITTING BOTTOM

We just kept struggling and fighting through bills. I finally got my big rig back at the end of November and went back to work in December. I couldn't get in or out of the truck without my brother-in-law's help because my back was still in such bad shape. I did that for the month of December, then Christmas break came and I was off until January. I worked until the end of January and went back for a doctor's appointment.

After his examination, the doctor basically said, "If you are going to stay driving that truck, don't come back and see me because you are going to end up in a wheel chair. I do not want to be a part of it. If you want me to help you, get out of the truck."

When I got home, I told Aurelie what the doctor said and I asked her, "If I can't do the work I have been doing, what am I going to do? That's what I do for a living. I own this truck and the truck has a $3,500.00 a month payment."

Aurelie looked at me and said, "Well, since you do not want to end up in a wheel chair, if the doctor says you are done, then you're done."

That was it. I was done. I let the truck go back to the leasing company that financed it. They were also suing us for thousands of dollars of unpaid monies. With no work, I had all the other bill collectors start calling again. Deeper and deeper I went down into the bottle. There was no relief as the vicious cycle continued.

Mom Is Diagnosed with Cancer

Mom and my stepdad had divorced because he was a closet alcoholic and she couldn't take it anymore. Several years later, Mom remarried again this time to a recovering alcoholic who had been sober for many years. Their relationship was solid and he was very good to her. Our family became very close with him over the years and began to trust him.

On September 17th a few years later, we found out my Mom had cancer. The carcinoma was in the final stages of the disease. The doctors projected that she maybe had a year left; at the best, maybe five years. Of course, we held on to the five-year plan. At the end of December of that year, just three months later, she went to be with Jesus.

The home they were living in needed renovations and I needed work so they hired me to build an addition for them. Since I was working there on the renovations, I got to spend quite a bit of time with her which I am so thankful for. I loved her so much. I was even able to drive her into Edmonton to the cancer clinic for her treatments. Then, only three and a half months after she was diagnosed, I was driving out to go visit her when I got the phone call that she passed away. Angry and grief stricken, I just put the pedal down. I was just looking for something to run into. I wanted to hit something so bad. I just wanted my car to explode and I wanted to be in it when it did. However, the road cleared and there was nothing I could hit, nothing. I just started punching the roof and screaming as I experienced that intense pain of grief and loss.

The funny thing is now I look back and I just thank God for my disability and being out of work at the time because I was able to spend a lot of quality time with my Mom. That day, though, I pulled that car over, slammed on the brakes, and jumped out of my car. Looking up at heaven, I shook my fist at God and just started hollering at Him, calling Him names, and swearing at Him trying to vent my anger and grief. I was so mad at Him. I couldn't believe that He had killed my mom and taken her away from me.

True to my pattern of handling pain and unpleasant circumstances, I drank even more. Aurelie sympathized with my loss. She saw me deteriorate and sink even further into an alcoholic depression. I didn't have a job, I broke my back, I was living in constant physical pain, and now my mom was dead. No good woman would complain about that, but I used it and abused it. I was now drinking like a mad man, never sober.

September of the following year, Aurelie's grandmother passed away. We went to the funeral then had to go back to our place and have a wake. You can't have a funeral if you're not going to get drunk afterwards. So I got drunk. That was on a Saturday. Sunday morning my wife's sister, who was up from British Columbia for the funeral, phoned her and asked her if she wanted to go to church with them. Aurelie said *yes*.

People often ask Aurelie what it was like living with an alcoholic husband. I believe you need to hear her side of this journey as well so I am going to give her a chance here to answer that question.

What Was It Like?

It was really tough because alcoholism wasn't something I was ever familiar with or exposed to like Shannon. I grew up on a farm where mom did all the cooking, the kids did chores, and dad did the field work.

Growing up I was definitely a rebellious child and I didn't like the word "no" much. When we got married, I went from living with my parents on a farm to living with Shannon in a city that was four hours away. That was hard. He would go out at night and I was home with a baby. I didn't know anybody in the town so I was really scared and alone. Shannon would come home so drunk he could not get his key in the lock, so I'd just sleep on the floor so I could buzz him in without waking any of the neighbors. We had many, many fights because I could not understand the alcoholism or even wrap my brain around why he could not overcome it.

Every time I heard a siren, I would worry that it would be him. Growing up I went to church, so when we hit this hard time I turned to God. Though I didn't have a relationship with Him, I turned to God when I really needed Him.

There was a lot of mistrust because I was always scared that he was out with not only alcohol but with other women. That wasn't the case, but there was unfaithfulness in my family so I didn't know for sure if Shannon was being faithful. Our kids were exposed to so much that they should have never ever seen. I have many regrets for that. There were many times I thought about leaving, but I was too scared to leave. There was also a part of me that took my vows seriously. I felt a marriage is forever. My parents went through a lot of garbage, but they still stayed married. Divorce wasn't something I was familiar with either.

We went through that for twenty years. We took our kids to church and we knew about God. We did everything that you are supposed to do as far as getting them baptized and confirmed, but we didn't stick around very long after that. In fact, as soon as our last daughter was confirmed the pastor looked at us and said, "I guess we won't be seeing you around anymore?" At first we kind of thought, "What a jerk," but he was absolutely right, we never did go back.

We never experienced growth or real fellowship within the church. Whether it was rebellion, fear of exposure or just lack of knowledge concerning what God could do as a real member of our family, we suffered as a family because of that.

However, God promises He will never leave us or forsake us.

For He Himself has said, "I will never leave you nor forsake you." (Hebrews 13:5)

Our lives are a testimony to the truth of that. We were so like the prodigal son who chose to go and live in the world until the world took everything and left us destitute and living in the midst of our own chosen pig pen. God never left us. In fact, like the father in the Parable of the Prodigal Son, He was waiting for us with open arms.

God the Father and the Prodigal Son

To illustrate the point further, Jesus told them this story: A man had two sons. The younger son told his father, "I want my share of your estate now before you die." So his father agreed to divide his wealth between his sons. A few days later this younger son packed all his belongings and moved to a distant land, and there he wasted all his money in wild living. About the time his money ran out, a great famine swept over the land, and he began to starve. He persuaded a local farmer to hire him, and the man sent him into his fields to feed the pigs. The young man became so hungry that even the pods he was feeding the pigs looked good to him. But no one gave him anything. When he finally came to his senses, he said to himself, "At home even the hired servants have food enough to spare, and here I am dying of hunger! I will go home to my father and say, 'Father, I have sinned against both heaven and you, and I am no longer worthy of being called your son. Please take me on as a hired servant.'" So he returned home to his father. And while he was still a long way off, his father saw him coming. Filled with love and compassion, he ran to his son, embraced him, and kissed him. His son said to him, "Father, I have sinned against both heaven and you, and I am no longer worthy of being called your son." But his father said to the servants, "Quick! Bring the finest robe in the house and put it on him. Get a ring for his finger and sandals for his feet. And kill the calf we have been fattening. We must celebrate with a feast, for this son of mine was dead and has now returned to life. He was lost, but now he is found." So the party began. (Luke 15:11-24 NLT)

When I read the story of the prodigal son, I saw so many parallels between our lives and that of the rebellious son, the father, and even the older brother Jesus talked about in Luke 15:11-32. When we were young, we wanted to immediately step into our inheritance without working to strengthen our character so we could withstand the temptations the world presented to us. The ways of the world were enticing and we thought we knew better than our parents.

The prodigal son probably felt his father was old fashion and out of touch with the real world. Like many young people today, we thought we knew more than our parents and did not want to embrace their lifestyle.

Shannon even vowed not become an alcoholic like his father. I went looking for love and acceptance in all the wrong places.

We chose to engage in worldly things and passions and found ourselves as young parents before we had matured sufficiently to handle the stress and responsibility of providing for a family.

Shannon thought he could just continue on selfishly indulging in his partying and all-night binges leaving me home with our young daughter. Because we had not really developed a solid relationship with each other putting God at the center of our marriage, I lived in loneliness and fear instead of feeling the security and protection God designed marriage to be for a man and a woman. When the stress or responsibility became too much for Shannon, he dove deeper into the alcoholism that eventually led him to the brink of suicide.

God designed marriage to be two people, a man and a woman, coming together as one flesh, complementing, supporting, and completing one another so they can build a safe and secure home to raise their children with God *first* in their relationship. Ecclesiastes 4:9-12 says, "Two people are better off than one, for they can help each other succeed. If one person falls, the other can reach out and help. But someone who falls alone is in real trouble. Likewise, two people lying close together can keep each other warm. But how can one be warm alone? A person standing alone can be attacked and defeated, but two can stand back-to-back and conquer. Three are even better, for a triple-braided cord is not easily broken."

Our prayer as we end this chapter of our story is that you have seen the benefit of building a relationship with God and with each other the way God designed marriage and family to be.

There is more to our story as we do indeed return to the waiting arms of our loving heavenly Father, but before we continue we would like to offer some suggestions for further study based on the truths we learned the hard way. Please take the time to go through this Digging Deeper section and apply these time proven truths in your own life.

Digging Deeper

Go back to the beginning and read God's original plan for marriage in Genesis 2:20b-25.

Why do you think there was no shame between Adam and his wife Eve?

Read what happened when Eve and then Adam decided they knew better than God and allowed themselves to be deceived and enticed by the devil in Genesis 3.

- *How did the serpent deceive the woman?*
- *Where was Adam?*
- *Why were they afraid when they heard God's voice calling them?*
- *What happened as a result of their disobedience to God's instructions?*
- *Have you disobeyed God's instructions?*
- *How has that worked out for you?*

Read the entire story Jesus told of the Prodigal Son in Luke 15:11-32.

- *What did this rebellious son discover about life out in the real world?*
- *What discovery have you made about the real world?*
- *What did this boy finally decide to do?*
- *What have you decided to do?*
- *Why do you think the father gave his son the inheritance he asked for?*
- *Why do you think God lets certain things happen in our lives?*
- *Are there changes you need to make in the way you are living your life?*
- *What is the first step you are going to take in the right direction?*

Begin by sitting down with God and asking Him to forgive you for your rebellion. Tell Him you know you have sinned against Him and you want to make things right. Ask Him to help you clean up your life. Write a brief prayer about this.

Chapter 4

INTO HIS WAITING ARMS

Sunday morning, my wife's sister who was up from BC for their grandmother's funeral, phoned Aurelie and asked her if she wanted to go to church. She immediately answered, "Yes!" Unbeknownst to me, she had been watching Hour of Power and a few other programs like that every once in a while just trying to figure out what life was all about and what was going on. I think God had started drawing her to Him a long time ago. She could hear Him and obeyed Him, though at the time she had no idea how this was all going to play out. One thing she did know, though, we could not keep going the way we were going or one or both of us would not make it. So after the phone call from her sister, Aurelie came and asked me if I wanted to go to church.

"Are you kidding me?" I asked her still drunk and hung over from the day before. "There is no way I want to go to any church!"

To make sure she really knew I meant it, I added some very explicit "words" to the end of my refusal. Aurelie went to the kids and told them she wanted them to go with her.

I started hollering at her to leave them alone and said, "You want to go to church, then you go yourself. You don't need us to go. Just because now all of a sudden you want to go, everybody's got to go?"

That brought back memories of when my dad used to take me to church once in a while. When I was growing up that was the best day of my life because it was the only day he didn't get drunk and beat somebody. Somehow, even his drunken eyes saw Sunday was a day to be respected and set apart.

God stepped in at that point and I decided to take a shower, so I yelled to Aurelie, "Get the kids ready. I'll drive you all to church, but I am not going in."

Even though I declared I was not going in, I got dressed up. We all piled into the car and headed for church. I thought I knew where the church was, but we ended up walking into the wrong church, realizing her sister was not there. Finally locating the right church, Aurelie and the kids quietly got out of the car.

"Wait," I surprised myself by saying, "I'll come in with you, but we are going to sit at the very back close to the door, and when that guy up front says amen, we are out of here. I'm not talking to anybody. I don't want to meet anybody. I don't want to visit with anybody."

Aurelie smiled and answered, "Deal."

So, we went in and sat at the back. I sat right on the outside of the pew that was closest to the door. My escape plan was in place. I figured I could make it out in about thirty seconds with no problem. These seats were just perfect. I even relaxed a little as they began their worship time. Everything was going just fine, and then the pastor started preaching. I have no idea what he preached about. I don't think I heard a word he said, but all of a sudden he had an altar call.

I found out later they did not always have an altar call, but that day they knew one of the member's had a son attending the service and they were all praying he would come up and give his life to the Lord. Little did any of them know that God had that altar call planned for a drunk, who still smelled like booze, and was hung over from a funeral.

All I knew was Jesus came and stood at the end of the pew. Somehow, I instinctively knew it was Him. He held His hand out to me and said, "Now is your time." He didn't have to explain it to me, He didn't have to write it down, He didn't have to draw me a picture. I knew it meant that I had to go now or I was going to die in my sin. I don't believe that it meant I was going to die that minute or keel over in the pew, but God looked at me that day and gave me a choice. I didn't have to think about it for very long. I got up and it was like I was holding His hand and Jesus was walking down the aisle with me. Though I had absolutely no idea what was going to happen, I wasn't scared or embarrassed.

I just walked right up to that pastor, he looked at me and said, "What can I do for you?"

"I don't know," I answered, "But I know I can't keep doing what I'm doing. I need help. I don't know what to do."

He asked, "Do you believe in God?"

"Yes," I answered emphatically.

"Do you believe that Christ died for your sins?"

Again I immediately answered, "Yes!"

"Then let's pray," and then he prayed with me.

I was ready to give my life to God. I was sick and tired of being sick and tired. I was over trying to fight through it all by myself. I just handed it over to God that day, I really truly did.

It still seems so unbelievable to me even now, because at that moment I was completely healed of the alcoholism. I was totally sober. I was no longer hung over. I couldn't even smell alcohol on me anymore.

I was cleansed from the inside out.

Incredibly happy, I turned around and walked back to the pew where the rest of my family was sitting. Aurelie was bawling like a baby and asked me if I would take her up to the altar.

Smiling broadly, I said, "Absolutely!"

Walking my wife up to the altar, I was like the proudest husband in the world. She gave her heart to the Lord that day, too. The kids thought we were crazy, but they were soon to see God was about to do amazing things in their parents. It's been an amazing journey ever since. Even though when we got home we still had bills to pay, we still owed lots of money, and we were still being sued, our outlook on life was totally changed. Nothing changed in the circumstance part of our world, but everything changed on inside of us. There wasn't fear any more of it. I didn't need to get drunk to try and deal with it. Instead, I read the Bible and prayed.

It was incredibly amazing because from that day on I was totally dedicated to the Lord.

Every day, I would walk through my house and pray. I would sit in my living room, read the Bible, pray, and then just close my eyes and let God speak to me. So many times He would show me visions and walk me to places only I would understand because He was talking to me in my language and in a way I could understand. He taught me how to trust Him and believe in Him for everything I needed. The places He took me and the things that He did were phenomenal.

Aurelie and I went to a Christian conference and the speaker there was talking about tithing and giving your all to God. We both looked at each other and felt a strong impression to give all we had. Well, all we had left to our name was $120 on our Visa and it was maxed. There were no more credit cards to use, they were all at their limits. There were no savings accounts, no money in the chequing account as it too had an overdraft that was maxed, and no other money to access from anywhere. As crazy as it may sound, we really felt we were called to give that $120. So, we filled in our Visa number on the offering envelope, gave our last dollars, and hoped for the best.

I decided to start making phone calls and try to clear up some debt. Every time I was ready to make a phone call, I would pray for wisdom and favor. Every place I called I would ask them about my debt, ask if there was anything they could do or if I could just make payments. I explained about my accident and that I really wanted to do something about the debt that wouldn't affect my credit rating. Every one of them settled for less. Whatever they settled for I could write that cheque that day and settle it.

I knew God had to be in on the whole thing.

The big one was my truck. We were getting sued for it. We ended up meeting with a lawyer out of Edmonton and told him how I had given it back, but now they were saying that it was in poor shape. Explaining I just had it all rebuilt in November after the accident, I told him I had given it back in February after driving it for just a few weeks in December and January. There is no way I could have worn it out that bad, especially since

I had such limited mobility myself. They were suing me for things that I didn't believe had anything to do with me.

The lawyer agreed to write them a letter and see what happens. I told him we had given our hearts to the Lord and we just prayed that this would get resolved for everyone. When I read the letter that he sent them, it said that our client prays to get this resolved and that they won't owe any money. It wasn't very long after that we received a copy of the letter the leasing company that was suing us sent to us and to our lawyer. I started reading the letter. It said the company was dropping all charges and not suing us. All they wanted from us was a promissory note saying we wouldn't counter sue them for falsely accusing us. I just fell to my knees and started to cry. Only God could have done something like that and we thanked Him for His provision and favor.

That was the way things happened as we went through bill by bill. It wasn't that we didn't have to do our part, but when we did God took care of the rest. It was like He was just waiting for us to turn to Him, take a step of faith, and honestly try to do what was right so He could pour out His blessings on us.

God went before us, softened hearts, and cleared the way for us each and every time.

The very last bill that we had was incredibly big, but we had seen God take us through each situation. It was almost like He was building our faith all along the way so we would be ready for this day. Our fuel bill for the truck was up to about eight thousand dollars. We drove up to the fuel company to take care of it in person. We were sitting in the pickup outside their office when I asked Aurelie how much money we had in the bank and she said there was $317.72. Though it was all we had, we agreed we would give it all to them as proof we wanted to begin making payments.

Then I walked into the office and said to the lady at the counter, "I want to make a payment on my account. I don't think I can pay it all off, but I would like to make a payment. Can you tell me what the balance is?"

She looked it up and then said, "Your balance is $317.72."

"I'll be right back," I said hardly believing my ears. "I have to get my chequebook out of the truck."

I went outside and told Aurelie what the woman had said. We could hardly believe it. We wrote that cheque for that amount, I took it in to the lady, and asked her to close my account because I could not drive truck anymore due to my accident.

The lady said, "Absolutely, Mr. Reeve, and thank you for your business."

Aurelie and I started to cry and praise God for His incredible love and provision! We truly saw Him make a way where there seemed to be no way through the mountains of debt we had accumulated through my foolish decisions and addictions.

So many times we worry about things. Since giving our lives to Christ, there are no **needs** in our life. They are all fulfilled. God has proven to be faithful in supplying our needs every time. All we had to do was learn to turn to Him first and desire to do things His way, the right way.

> *"Therefore do not worry, saying, 'What shall we eat?' or 'What shall we drink?' or 'What shall we wear?' For after all these things the Gentiles seek. For your heavenly Father knows that you need all these things. But seek first the kingdom of God and His righteousness, and all these things shall be added to you. Therefore do not worry about*

tomorrow, for tomorrow will worry about its own things. Sufficient for the day is its own trouble. (Matthew 6:31-34)

Digging Deeper

Read the following scriptures and choose this day whom you will serve.

John 14:6 says Jesus is _____

John 8:32 says His truth will _____

John 3:16-18 says God sent His Son, Jesus to _____

John 16:33 says, Jesus He has overcome the _____ to give us _____

John 14:27 says Jesus gives us _____

Just like it was time for Shannon to make a choice, it is time for you to choose as well. Jesus is standing at the door of your heart asking you to take His hand and walk from darkness to light, from fear to peace, and from death to life. Will you choose Him today?

Say this simple prayer asking God to forgive you of your sins. Then accept the gift God gives you through His Son, Jesus.

Father God, I know I have not lived my life the right way. I have sinned and need Your forgiveness. Thank You for sending Your Son to die for me, to take my punishment, and to make a way to eternal life. I ask You to help me to now move forward with my life. I desire to please and serve You the rest of my days and to do things the right way, Your way. Today I choose You!

Chapter 5

GOD'S PLAN FOR MY LIFE

All we like sheep have gone astray; we have turned, every one, to his own way; and the Lord has laid on Him the iniquity of us all. (Isaiah 53:6)

It has been an amazing journey. When I look back at all the time, effort, and money I wasted on alcohol and drugs, I am truly saddened. I am so thankful God never turned His back on me though I chose to turn my back on Him and even accused Him of taking things I love from me. The truth was, though I loved Aurelie, my kids, my mom, and my grandparents, I was living in a self-centered, self-focused mode with no real regard for other people's stuff. I would even steal from people I loved. I would take money out of my mother's purse. I broke into houses, would steal guns, and did so many other foolish things when I was younger. If it wasn't for God's hand on my life, I probably would not have lived through my teenage years.

I had a friend I hung out with that was just as crazy as I was. We would go together and break into the houses of people he babysat for after he'd scoped out the house and left a window unlocked. We had all these plans of stealing cars and then driving around shooting out the back windows of parked cars or shooting at cops. I actually never shot a gun in my life. It's amazing how these thoughts get into your head. I always wanted to be a gangster, or so I thought. Can you imagine a twelve or thirteen-year old shooting out the window of a stolen car? We target practiced in the basement with a 22. The thing would be ricocheting all over the place so we would duck behind a mattress. We could hear that bullet ricocheting all over, but never considered what would happen if we were actually hit with one of them.

One of the funny things about those times was we would run away all the time when we thought our moms were mean to us by making us do our homework and chores and stuff. We lived in the city of Edmonton on the west end and there was lots of brush areas on the one side of Mayfield Road. There was no development there yet and we would run into the brush and hide out all the time.

One time we made it all the way to the south side which was actually a long way away from the west end where we lived. This time we had the police looking for us. We were doing good setting up our camp by making our beds from boughs we cut off the spruce trees. We were going to stay there forever, but then it got dark. We started to talk about how this wasn't the right thing to do to our moms, so we decided to phone home and get a ride back from which ever mom answered our call. I don't know how I lived to be fourteen, never mind beyond that to become an alcoholic drug abuser.

It's just so amazing to me that God brought me through all of that because He had a purpose for my life.

And we know that all things work together for good to those who love God, to those who are the called according to His purpose. (Romans 8:28)

God's Protection

After Aurelie and I became Christians, all the fun started. We went to meetings all over the place because we didn't want to miss anything God was doing. We went to prophetic meetings once we found out what they were all about. I wanted to get there before some friends of ours did because I didn't want anyone to have the opportunity to tell the speaker anything about me. When this prophet spoke over me, I knew there was no way anybody could have shared any of what he told me. He knew all about my back injury, the accident, and even my drug and alcohol abuse. Then he told me what God wanted for me.

> *For I know the thoughts that I think toward you, says the LORD, thoughts of peace and not of evil, to give you a future and a hope.* (Jeremiah 29:11)

It's not that everything was rosy during this time, either. I still didn't have a job, but it was obvious God was working in our lives. There were lots of really good moments and some we did not understand at the time. Then there was an odd one where Aurelie and I didn't see eye to eye in what we felt God was saying. It happened when we were still immature in Christ and did not realize that He speaks to me differently than He speaks to Aurelie because we are two different people. We were learning to grow and mature in Him. Just like in our natural bodies, we had to endure some growing pains along the way.

God knows how He needs to deal with each one of us. He will say the same thing, but He may not say it the exact same way.

Then I went through a time where I could see demons. They were all over the place. They were just short little guys with black gowns and black hoods. I actually thought it was cool that I could walk into a place, see people's demons, pray for them, and cast them out. So, I did that for a couple of years. Then all of a sudden that ability to see demons went away.

I was upset and said to God, "I thought you gave me a gift where I could see people's evil spirits and I could pray for them."

He just said to me so clearly, "What makes you think that those were other people's spirits?"

That's when I realized that those were my own demons. They were legions just waiting for an opportunity to come back on me, but they were uninvited so they could not. I'm glad to say that I don't see them anymore, and I don't want to, now that I understand what they were doing.

> *Keep awake! Watch at all times. The devil is working against you. He is walking around like a hungry lion with his mouth open. He is looking for someone to eat. Stand against him and be strong in your faith. Remember, other Christians over all the world are suffering the same as you are. (1 Peter 5:8-9)*

Another incident happened in the winter when I went with a buddy of mine to go check trap lines. We drove from his place taking two sleds on a trailer. We got to a spot I had never been to before and unloaded the sleds. He showed me where he put the keys to the truck just in case I needed to get them. He actually put them in where the gas cap is located. He started drinking. I'll be honest, I had a couple of drinks throughout the day because he kept pressuring me. He kept wanting me to drink with him. Mostly, I was just pouring coke into my glass.

We got to the cabin and unloaded all of our gear and then fired up the generator and got a fire going. Then we went out to check the trap line. He was still drinking and kept telling me to drink. I would fill my cup up with coke instead. When we got back to the cabin, he realized I wasn't drinking and started getting madder and madder at me.

We were sitting at the table in the cabin talking, and he kept trying to force me to drink. Then he started getting weird on me and kind of making passes at me in a sexual way. He was doing things that really started to freak me out. I'm praying God would get me through this. I really did not understand what was going on. I had known this guy for a long time and partied with him several times, but nothing like this ever happened before. He kept persisting and persisting.

Finally, for some reason I looked at his hands. They were all red and chapped. I asked him about it. He said he had eczema really bad on his hands and it really bothered him. Without even thinking about it, I asked him if I could pray for his hands. He said, "Yes," so I did I put my hand over top of his and prayed that the eczema would be gone in Jesus name. When I said amen I looked at him and his face changed. Then I knew it wasn't him sitting there anymore. He started getting really miserable.

He looked me in the eyes with a cold hard stare and said, "You're bigger than David." Satan had entered this man and the battle was about to begin. All of a sudden, he got up and walked over to the kitchen sink. When he turned around and started walking back toward me, he had a butcher knife in his hand. I didn't even get a chance to ask him what he was doing with that knife, when the generator ran out of gas. The lights went out and that was just enough to throw him off. He threw the knife back towards the kitchen sink.

I quickly said, "Don't worry, I'll run out and take care of it."

Putting my outdoor gear on, I went out and put about a gallon of gas in the generator, just enough to get some lights back on. I was scared and wanted to put the rest of the gas in my sled and get out of there. I started to head toward my sled with the gas can, trying to avoid the light from the cabin door. Inside the cabin, my friend was flipping the bunk beds and tearing the place apart like a mad man. He looked up and saw me and asked me what I was doing. I told him I was just gassing up the sleds so we wouldn't have to do it in the morning. Then I asked him what he was doing.

"I'm looking for my gun," he said. "I keep a gun here."

I just freaked out. As soon as my sled was full, I flung the gas can as far away as I could, put the gas cap on my sled, fired it up, and I was gone. I went about fifty yards from the cabin and realized I had no idea where I was and I was scared. I knew I couldn't stay there because I wasn't far enough away from that cabin. I had to get away from there since for some reason, "my friend" wanted to kill me.

I looked up and said, "God, I don't even know if I'm going in the right direction. I'm just going to hold this thing wide open and go. When you want me to turn, I'll turn."

I would be going fast and suddenly, my hand would come off the throttle just as I came to a corner and I would just turn. It happened time and time again. I'd go full out and all of a sudden my hand would come off and I'd turn. Now if anybody's ever been sledding before, you know it is hard enough to get your bearing during the day, when you are somewhere you have only been through once. Night time is way different then during the day. I would turn the corner and I would look up again and pray. Finally, I got down to where we came off the river, but I couldn't cross the river right there because of ice piled up. I couldn't see where we came down the other side because it was too dark.

So, I just looked up again at God and said, "I'm just going to hold this thing to the boards and when You want me to turn, I'll turn, but I'm not stopping until then."

I had that thing wide open. All of a sudden I felt to turn, and when I did I could see the trail going up the bank. I went across the river, went up the bank, and was within ten feet of his truck. I turned the sled off, left the keys in it, got the keys out of the gas tank, and took his truck. I went back to his place got in my truck and left. I phoned Aurelie on my way home. It was about four in the morning. I was so scared that my body was trembling in fear. I told her I was just totally freaked out. When I got home and I was still shaking.

Aurelie says, "He was white as a ghost and the look of fear in his eyes was unlike anything I had ever seen."

We sat down together and I recalled all the events of the evening. During this time our youngest daughter woke up, heard the commotion, and came downstairs to see what was going on. Seeing the fear in her father's eyes, she became very concerned and asked what was wrong with Daddy. Not wanting to alarm or scare her, Aurelie took her back to bed and reassured her everything was going to be okay.

I was so scared that whenever our cat would walk by me and I would just come out of my skin. Finally, about eight in the morning, Aurelie phoned her work and told them that we had a family emergency and that she would not be in, then she called our pastor and told him what was going on. He and his wife came out right away and they started praying for us. Then we went around and prayed over all our doors, doorways, windows, and basically prayed the blood of Jesus all over our house. Every once in a while I would go upstairs to the bathroom and splash cold water on my face trying to snap out of it. I just could not stop shaking. They prayed for me for hours.

Finally, I went and splashed cold water on my face. As I looked in the mirror and saw the frightened expression on my face, I prayed, God, I want this to be over!"

God said, "Alright, go get dressed and it is finished."

I went over, got dressed, went downstairs, and looked at Aurelie, the pastor and his wife. They were all still praying.

I simply said, "Okay guys, we are done. God just told me it's finished."

They went home, and the rest of the evening I was fine. The next day, Aurelie went to work, insisting that in the event my friend showed up I would not answer the door. Fearing for what might happen if I did. A few hours later, I looked out the living room window and all of a sudden a pickup pulls into the yard. God must have prepared my heart because I had no fear or anxiety when he walked up to our door. I opened the door and asked him in.

He just looked at me and asked, "What happened? When I woke up and you weren't there I realized something went horribly wrong. Did I do something stupid? If I did, I just wanted to come and apologize."

I kind of explained to him a little of what happened. He promised me he would quit drinking, but unfortunately I don't think that he did. Needless to say, we never went hunting or off together ever again.

I was learning to trust God and at the same time learning how much Satan is out to get us. He will use whatever and whomever and will basically stop at nothing to try and take us out. The difference in my life now was I knew God was there with a plan. He was not going to let the enemy anywhere near me as long as I called upon the name of Jesus and stayed connected to Him.

> *Put on the things God gives you to fight with. Then you will not fall into the traps of the devil.* ***Our fight is not with***

> *people. It is against the leaders and the powers and the spirits of darkness in this world. It is against the demon world that works in the heavens. Because of this, put on all the things God gives you to fight with. Then you will be able to stand in that sinful day. When it is all over, you will still be standing. So stand up and do not be moved. Wear a belt of truth around your body. Wear a piece of iron over your chest which is being right with God. Wear shoes on your feet which are the Good News of peace. Most important of all, you need a covering of faith in front of you. This is to put out the fire-arrows of the devil. The covering for your head is that you have been saved from the punishment of sin. Take the sword of the Spirit which is the Word of God.* (Ephesians 6:11-17 emphasis added)

Digging Deeper

I was learning to trust God and at the same time learning how much Satan is out to get us. He will use whatever and whomever, and will basically stop at nothing to try and take us out. The difference in my life now was I knew God was there with a plan. He was not going to let the enemy anywhere near me as long as I called upon the name of Jesus and stayed connected to Him.

In John 10:10, what did Jesus say about the enemy's plan?
What did He say about why He came?
What does Ephesians 6:11-17 say about the type of warfare we have to fight?
What weapons has God given us to fight this battle?
What does James 4:7 tell us to do when the devil comes along?

Read how Jesus dealt with the devil when He was in the wilderness right after His baptism in Matthew 4:1-11. What did you learn about how to handle the devil from Jesus?

Pray and ask God to give you wisdom each time the devil comes your way and tries to tempt you to do something you know would not please God. Remember to use all of the weapons God has given you and God will see you through each battle.

So give yourselves to God. Stand against the devil and he will run away from you. (James 4:7)

Chapter 6

AURELIE'S WALK WITH JESUS

The Lord is my light and the One Who saves me. Whom should I fear? The Lord is the strength of my life. Of whom should I be afraid? (Psalm 27:1)

Getting saved, I remember a presence coming to live inside me that wasn't there before.

Prior to going to church that Sunday, I remember when I went to sleep at night dark shadows would cast over me. Then I thought I'd best get my affairs in order, and do the things I wanted to do for my children because I was going to die soon feeling or thinking it was the angel of death. The day I gave my heart to Jesus those shadows vanished.

When we started going to church on a regular basis I was so excited, but then Shannon and I would end up fighting afterwards. I would get angry and have this attitude of why bother going if this is what happens every time after we go to church. Surprisingly after a couple of times, Shannon identified that it was the enemy trying to keep us from going and we would resist the forces of evil and go to church anyways. Hearing my husband say things like that was wonderful, but I remember wondering if this was for real and going to last.

Is This for Real?

My husband had changed drastically and I was falling in love with this new man all over again. Lots of times I look at my husband and wonder what I ever did to be blessed with such an incredible man, which is the exact opposite of what I used to think when he was out all night drinking and I was home alone with our three children. I had said countless prayers in our early married life asking for Shannon to quit drinking. Now that he had, for a while I have to admit, I still wondered if it was for real and if he could really quit something he had been addicted to all his life cold turkey like that.

It was real. Not only had Shannon quit drinking, he was praying, and reading his Bible! He was becoming an amazing man of God, a man after God's own heart. Shannon has never been one that likes to read, yet the wisdom that came out of him lined up with God's Word. God met Shannon right where he was and taught him how he needed to be taught in a way that he could understand. Attending church became the highlight of my week! Through the years I have learned that I have a heart of worship and could sing praises all day every day. That is truly my happy place. I have even had the privilege of being on a worship team.

Shannon drew closer and closer to God each passing day. He was very quick to love when anger between the two of us arose. He could quickly identify when the enemy was at work trying to get between us. Once he said the devil was doing it and I took it as if he was calling me the devil. Of course, he was not. He matured quicker than I did. It was kind of like when Jesus said to Peter, "Get behind Me, Satan!" (Matthew 16:23). Jesus was not calling Peter Satan. He was speaking to the influence of the enemy that was trying to cause a separation between them.

Our kids were also confused. We went from party hardy to being radical for Christ. Though they were passed the Sunday school age, they would come to church with us. Our oldest was attending college so she didn't attend all the time. I think everyone we knew and used to hang out with thought we had fallen off the deep end. Many friendships were lost as we embraced our new love for the Lord.

We took a couple of our kids with us to a Christian conference and I got angry with them because they were just sitting there like bumps on a log. They were not willing to participate in anything and were mad at us for bringing them there. With their attitude painfully obvious, I started talking to God and asked Him what was going on with them and why they didn't get it.

All of a sudden a very strong voice spoke to me saying, "What makes you think you are so special?"

"Pardon me?" confused, I asked the Voice.

"I came and got you when you were thirty-five years old," He said. "What makes you think I am not coming to get your kids, too?"

Yikes, I had been scolded by my heavenly Father! It humbled me greatly. I was trying to make my kids turn their hearts to Him which is His job, not mine. So now I sit back and I trust, well, at least I try to. Every once in a while I try to take over only to realize it is not me that does the calling, it is Him. I still struggle with lots of my children's activities, but I know that God can work all things together for those that love Him. I stand on His Word and declare, "As for me and my house we will serve the Lord." He has promised me that He will come and get them, too. I have to either believe all of the Bible and His promises or none of it is real in my life.

For by grace you have been saved through faith, and that not of yourselves; it is the gift of God. (Ephesians 2:8)

However, that doesn't mean we didn't face battles along the way. Satan moved quickly and created a lot of chaos between us and our children. The day we were baptized, one of our children stormed out of the house and did not speak to us for weeks. That was so incredibly hard to handle. We were very close with our children and Satan knew exactly how to hit us below the belt.

However, our walk was real and that was what our kids needed to see. We continued to walk with Christ, reading the Bible and trying to learn what God's intention for our lives was despite our circumstance. Eventually, our children realized this was the real deal and we were not going back to the way things were. They slowly began to accept these new parents.

He has shown you, O man, what is good; and what does the LORD require of you but to do justly, to love mercy, and to walk humbly with your God. (Micah 6:8)

A Miracle

One weekend we went on a quadding trip with some friends of ours. It was an August weekend that was hot and beautiful outside so I didn't want to wear my helmet. Later, I would learn why they were so important. We had been quadding down the shallow water on the edge of a river rock bed. It was so much fun! There was water spraying everywhere, and on a hot day it felt awesome.

Shannon, his brother-in-law, our nephew, And Ben, Shannon's friend, and me were the group. They all went up the side of the river bank and away we went. Shannon waited at the top for me. I was hesitant and scared, but my pride won over. I couldn't let all these men show me up. So, I geared up and away I went, attempting to scale the wall of the river bed. Well, I didn't make it. I got part way up, and then it was like time stood still. All of a sudden, I was falling backwards.

My head hit the rocks and then the quad came crashing down on top of me. I remember the sound of my head hitting the rocks and then this large quad landing on my face. I was hurt, but conscious. My eyes were closed, but I could hear mumbling sounds in the distance. Gaining some control over my functions, I worked my way up to my knees and just prayed, "God, please don't let me be blind."

Slowly, I started opening my eyes. Thankfully, I could see, but what I saw was very disturbing. There was blood all over the rocks, my blood. Dizzy at first, everything else began to come into focus. The guys had surrounded me and were lifting the quad off me.

Shannon kept asking, "Babe, are you okay?"

At first, I could not respond. He got me up to my feet, but when they saw all the blood and knew I had hit my head, they knew I had to get to the hospital as quickly as possible. The guys got my quad up the embankment. Shannon got me on his quad and the others all mounted theirs. Ben stopped everyone and said we needed to pray. The ride out of there seemed so incredibly long, but finally we got to our vehicles. Shannon got me into his truck and we were gone in a flash. I have no idea how fast he was going, but I remember feeling like we were gliding.

Finally, we arrived at the hospital, but we were concerned that because it was a long holiday weekend there might only be a skeleton staff working. Thanks to the God we serve, there was a doctor and an x-ray technician there. God is so good. They examined me, pulled the glass out of my face from the glasses I was wearing, and gave me stitches under my eye. Other than that, they said the rest were just bumps and bruises.

However, a few days later my hand was really hurting so we went to our hometown hospital and they took an x-ray of it. The technician was so mad at me because I couldn't get my wedding rings off. I would learn later the significance of them being in my x-rays. The doctor confirmed the break, but told me I had to wait for a bit of the swelling to go down so they could cast it.

Three days later, we were on the way back for them to put on the cast when Shannon prayed that when they went to take another x-ray, the break would be gone and I would be healed. Well, they took another x-ray and sure enough they couldn't find the break. They called in an x-ray expert to look at the new x-ray as well and compare the two. There was no doubt it was the right x-ray because there were my wedding rings. They came to us and said they didn't know what happened but that break was gone. Shannon told them we knew what happened, we had prayed! The technicians even put in the report that the patient prayed and when the new x-rays were taken, the break was apparently healed.

> *Trust in the LORD with all your heart, and lean not on your own understanding; In all your ways acknowledge Him, and He shall direct your paths.* (Proverbs 3:5-6)

Life after Meeting Christ

Shannon and I have been through so very much through the thirty-three years that we have been together. The first nineteen years of our lives together were very volatile and unsteady, with a lot of drinking, drugs, and fighting. We were fairly confident that there were bets on the table when we got married that we would never last.

In fact, a family member even phoned us on our fifth anniversary, and when he was talking to Shannon he said, "Congratulations! I always knew you'd be married for five years."

Shannon beamed and said, "Awe, thanks man!"

Then there was a giggle on the other end of the phone and the man said, "I just didn't think it would be to the same woman!"

Sure there were a lot of good times, but there were a lot of bad that we both regret. We would have raised our family so very differently if only we had known better. We feel like our children have seen so much stuff that we should have been protecting them from, not displaying in front of them.

When we gave our hearts to the Lord, there were many skeletons we had to deal with that had accumulated in our lives over the years and caused problems between the two of us. God's Word says if we confess our sins one to another we will be forgiven and that if we trust in the Lord with all our heart and all our soul and lean not on our own understanding, He will direct our path and lead us in the way we should go. I didn't know how true these scriptures were until we were tested.

If we confess our sins, He is faithful and just to forgive us our sins and to cleanse us from all unrighteousness. (1 John 1:9)

Was it easy to share the deepest darkest places of our hearts with each other? Not at all. It took many days of prayer for me to work up the nerve to actually carry through with it when the Holy Spirit revealed an area I had to confess to Shannon. However, once it was said it was too late to take it back. Each time I followed the guidance of the Holy Spirit, by the grace of God we were able to work through everything. What Satan meant for harm, Jesus forgave us of and we forgave each other as well. Today, we are closer than ever. In fact, Shannon is my very best friend. We have such a trust between us that we can come to each other for whatever is burdening our hearts and know we will not be judged. We have learned the powerful truth of what Jesus said in Matthew 6:14-15.

"If you forgive people their sins, your Father in heaven will forgive your sins also. If you do not forgive people their sins, your Father will not forgive your sins."

Tests of Our Faith

We came to love our church family like they were our own. God blessed us with friends that still are there for us today. Despite the closure of our church, we have remained very close with many of these people. They have been there for us through so much and I thank God for each and every one of them. Joni has been my friend in my deepest darkest times, my prayer warrior when needed, and an amazing example of a godly woman on a regular basis. She is beautiful inside and out. She has always been there for me, even when I didn't realize I needed her.

One of the biggest events that tested my faith was the death of our first grandchild. Our middle daughter was married and they were expecting our very first grandchild. We all were so very excited. In the first trimester, some tests were completed that indicated there were several things very wrong with this child and they were advised they should abort the pregnancy. They were in shock. Abortion was never something they had ever believed in, so of course, the answer was an instant and emphatic, "No!"

Our daughter and her husband had started attending church with us, and I felt God was doing a work in their lives through this decision.

The doctors told them that because they had made the decision to have the child in spite of their advice, there would have to be a specialist team of about fifteen people to be ready to act when our granddaughter was born.

We believed God would take care of everything. Many people prayed for this little one, day after day, right up until the day she was born.

That day is forever etched in my mind. Laurie was finally in labor. Excited with anticipation, we rushed to the hospital to be there for the big event. Hours went by. At one point, the doctor became a bit concerned because baby's heart beat was slower than normal. I took my cell phone and put worship music on and placed it on Laurie's tummy. The baby's heart beat increased. Laurie went in on Tuesday and by Thursday the baby still had not arrived. They had jelled Laurie four times to try and force labor which we found out later was a dangerous course of action as it can cause the placenta to pull away from the child.

Finally, it was happening. The contractions were very close together and it was time for the baby to come. We were outside her delivery room, and all of a sudden we could tell something was wrong, very wrong. They were desperately looking for the doctor, who had just been there, but was suddenly nowhere to be found. They rushed our daughter off to do an emergency caesarian.

We were in shock and had no idea at this point what had happened. About an hour later, we were in the waiting room with Calvin, the baby's father, when the doctor came out and told us what had happened. A little baby girl, our little Kaelyn, had been born, but the placenta had pulled away and she was without oxygen for eighteen minutes. She was now on life support. Not only that, they had to give our daughter a blood transfusion as she had lost a lot of blood and they almost lost her on the operating table.

Our minds were reeling. Where was this team of fifteen specialists that was supposed to be there? Where did the doctor go right when everything went wrong?

When we asked the doctor why he hadn't taken the baby the day before, his reply was, "Hind sight is 20/20."

That was all he said and then he walked away. In desperation, we were on the phone instantly begging everyone for prayer. Then we had to deal with different doctors telling Calvin to pull the plug on the life support. Laurie wasn't even out of the operating room yet. He said he was not going to make that decision without consulting with his wife.

Finally, we were all able to go and see Laurie and tell her the horrible news. It was awful. As parents, we felt utterly helpless. We spent time with Calvin and Laurie and precious moments with Kaelyn while she was still alive. For as adamant as they were about them taking her off life support, we are fairly confident they decided to end her life. They told us they thought she was having a seizure and were going to give her medication for it. Once they did that, she took her last breath. The rest of the evening we spent holding her and saying our goodbyes.

"How could this be?" I asked God, my mind was racing a million miles a minute. "Kaelyn was prayed for. I trusted You! You can raise her still!"

I remember even when we were burying her thinking, *God, it is not too late You can still raise her*. But nothing happened, at least not what we wanted to happen.

This event rocked my faith and made me question if there was even a God. My spirit was so crushed I wouldn't play or sing my worship music.

Now faith is the substance of things hoped for, the evidence of things not seen. (Hebrews 11:1)

Shannon was a rock and his faith remained steadfast. He still felt God was in control. At this point, I didn't want to have anything to do with this God that didn't answer so many prayers. It was probably the only time I was angry at Shannon for trusting God. However, God is faithful and He still loved me even when I turned my back on Him. He nursed my broken heart, and brought me back to Him. I don't have the why, but I know the only pain Kaelyn ever experienced was her first twelve hours of life, and then she went to be with the Father for a life that was far better than earth could have ever offered her.

My daughter asked why God took her. My answer was God didn't take her, but I know He received her. We live in a fallen world and sometimes doctors make wrong choices and there are consequences to those choices.

There were many difficult moments after that, but God held all of our hands and hearts through it all!

Never Alone by Barlow Girl became the first worship song I sang after losing Kaelyn. Finally, the spirit of worship was alive in me again. It took a long time for me to sing any worship songs, but once God had healed my broken heart, I found myself beginning to talk to God through music once again. Lyrics from a song were constantly running through my head, then to my heart, and finally my vocal chords. *I waited for you today, but you didn't show... I needed you today, so where did you go? He had told me countless times that I could call and that He would be there.... But where was He...was my God, my creator, my only reason for living there?* This song spoke volumes to me. It found me right where I was at. I couldn't see, feel, or hear my Lord and began to even doubt His existence, but through His faithfulness He taught me that He was there. I was never alone and He revived in me the deep reassurance He had placed in my life a long time ago. He will not separate from me, He is my creator. He was invisible, but after time I learned to trust what I could not see.

I am thankful that my God can handle everything I have ever given Him. The anger, forgiveness, the doubt, and countless other negative emotions has never affected God's love for me. I will always trust the unseen.

We now have seven alive and well beautiful grandchildren, but Kaelyn is never far from our hearts or our thoughts. We will all have to wait to find out the why, but for now we will trust that God is and always will be in control. His ways are higher than ours and He is the only one who knows the end from the beginning concerning all of our lives.

Well, that happened more than eight years ago and we are still walking with our Lord. I still question Him from time to time, but He is faithful and loving in helping me to walk through it. I try hard to understand His Word and what it is He calls me to do, but when I lack understanding I trust, worship, and try to draw near to Him.

Come close to God and He will come close to you. (James 4:8)

Closure of the Church

Another upsetting thing for us was the closure of our church. Some things were going on that we did not feel were of God and we could no longer be under that leadership. We prayed about it and felt God told us it was time for us to leave. However, we never thought for a moment the church would end up closed. We were just going to wait for the leadership to leave and then we would go back. We tried attending different churches, but nowhere did we feel at home like we did in the church where we gave our hearts to Jesus. After the church closure, we had church at home. It wasn't the same for sure. I missed our church family terribly, but things were different now, nothing was as it was. We wandered around in the desert for quite a few years trying to find our place in this world. God was faithful during our wilderness wanderings and never left our sides.

Perhaps it was our time to study to show ourselves approved by God without the interference of man's opinions and input. Like Paul, we needed to focus on the Word of God and learn to follow the leading of the Holy Spirit (see Galatians 1:15-24).

Shannon's Illness

Shannon had been having incredible dizzy spells. We went to many doctor appointments trying to figure out what was wrong with him. Some days it was so bad, I would have to drive him where he needed to go. The doctor treated him for so many different things, but nothing was working.

Finally, the doctor told us that he had treated Shannon with everything for dizziness possible, the only other thing it could be was a tumor in his brain. So, he wanted to send Shannon for an MRI to see where the tumor was. I was so scared and so was Shannon. A couple of weeks went by prior to the MRI appointment. For months, I had been getting up on weekdays at 6:00 a.m. to read my Bible. Weekends I would sleep in.

The Saturday of the MRI appointment, God woke me up at 6 a.m. and told me to go read my Bible. I struggled with Him for a bit because I wanted to sleep in, but He eventually won and I got out of bed and headed to my Bible. For about ten minutes, I sat reading the story about Solomon in 1 Kings. Not finding anything relevant and finding it hard to stay awake, I started asking God *why* He gotten me up to read so early.

Then I heard, "Go back and read it over again."

So I went back and started reading again and suddenly I saw, "Ask for what you want."

> *At Gibeon the LORD appeared to Solomon in a dream by night; and God said, "Ask! What shall I give you?* (1 Kings 3:5)

That is what God had told Solomon and was now telling me to do as well.

I said, "Well, I know the right thing to ask for is wisdom, as the Word tells me."

"Ask for what you want," came the command once again.

"It isn't wisdom I want," I admitted. "I am asking for Shannon's health."

Then it was quiet. Later, we went to the appointment as scheduled. The next morning, Sunday morning, the doctor phoned us at home to tell us the MRI was clear and that there was **no tumor**. First of all, the doctor phoned us on a Sunday, no doctor ever does that! Then we find out there was no tumor. We instantly thanked God and the excitement in us bubbled over.

We have been through many difficult trials and tribulations. I am still learning to praise God even in the storm. I don't know if I will ever get that right all the time, but I am so thankful that God is faithful and because He is love He is there for me and always will be.

> *It is done. I am the Alpha and the Omega, the Beginning and the End. To him who is thirsty I will give to drink without cost from the spring of the water of life. He who overcomes will inherit all this, and I will be his God and he will be my son.* (Revelation 21:6-7)

Digging Deeper

Perhaps like us, you have been through many difficult trials and tribulations.

What did Jesus tell us about trials and tribulations in John 16:33?

How does Proverbs 23:7 help us in dealing with trials and tribulations?

What does Romans 8:37 promise?

What is God's promise to us in 1 Corinthians 10:13?

What is the promise from God in Joshua 1:5 and Hebrews 9:22?

I am still learning to praise God even in the storm. I don't know if I will ever get that right all the time, but I am so thankful that God is faithful and because He is love He is there for me and always will be. He is there for you as well.

Pray and thank God for being with you through every trial, tribulation, and storm. Remember to praise Him even in the midst of your storm. You will be amazed at what happens when you do!

Chapter 7

OUR DAUGHTERS' STORIES

Children's children are the crown of old men; and the glory of children are their fathers. (Proverbs 17:6 KJV)

Stefanie

Stefanie is our oldest daughter and the one who had the hardest time with all that our family went through before we gave our lives to Christ. She agreed to share her thoughts so here is her story.

Did you know that one in five adults have lived with an alcoholic relative while growing up? I am part of that statistic. My dad was an alcoholic. I was asked what life was like growing up with an alcoholic parent. To be honest, at the time I didn't know any different, so my answer is normal. I thought that was what life was like and maybe I still do. Truth is I don't think I am any different than him.

I remember I always felt lonely. I could never have a best friend. We moved so much it was hard to maintain any friendships. Dad was always chasing work. Was this due to alcohol? I don't know as those kinds of things were not discussed with us or around us much.

My mom and dad fought a lot, though. Naturally, when I heard them fighting I wanted to find a way to listen to what was going on. So, I'd slip down the hallway, tiptoe to the steps, drop into a tight crouch on the landing, and peer over my knees at my curled-up toes. I imagine I must have looked like a gargoyle crouching there on the landing trying to listen to what they were arguing about. Though, I guess I was not a very effective gargoyle because I couldn't seem to keep the house free of bad stuff. Sometimes their arguments would last for hours, so eventually, I would go back to bed and just cry myself to sleep.

The one vision I will never forget was watching my mom pack my dad's stuff along with the Nintendo (the things we remember as kids). Anyway, she cried as she packed boxes of his stuff. As I remember she had given him an ultimatum and was following through when he did not do what she had asked. It probably had to do with the alcoholism. All I know is it broke my heart to see her crying like that.

I have always thought of my dad as a great man, though. I watched him as I was growing up. He taught me about hard work and providing for your family and for that I am forever grateful.

When I was asked what God has done for my parents, I first thought of when my grandma died. I believe that as my dad lost a part of himself when he lost my grandma, he also found himself. Maybe it was grandma's gift to him.

Then I remembered that my mom and dad once posted what they felt God has done to them. I believe that this describes it very well.

He has enlightened what's dark in them, strengthened what's weak in them, mended what's broken in them, bound what's bruised in them, healed what's sick in them, and lastly, He has revived whatever peace and love that had died in them.

They are inspiring and they believe in me even when I don't.
I love you both,
-*Stefanie Reeve*

Laurie

As the daughter of an alcoholic, you would think my story would come with some sort of sad childhood remembrances, and many probably do. Mine, however, proves just how secretive an addict can be. I really had no idea.

It was not until my adult years that I learned of my father's battles with alcohol. Being on the other side of it now, I am not filled with anger or resentment, but rather sadness and sympathy. The hurt he hid in every bottle must have been unimaginable, which brings me to how proud and thankful I am for him. Like many other alcoholics, he could have left us, beat us, or beat our mother. Instead, he kept his suffering mostly to himself. By mostly I mean, I remember the arguments between my parents. Some were worse than others.

There is only one time I personally recall being directly affected by his drinking. It was a night after they had been out partying, like many other nights. We used to laugh and think we were lucky to have such easy going parents. This night, my dad was in the kitchen with a drink in hand. I had already helped my mom upstairs and to bed. I went to him and attempted to dump his drink, and let him know he'd had too much. Looking back, I realize now that was a bad idea. I remember his yelling and me crying. I remember leaving him with his drink and going to bed thinking, *What an* ____.

However, by the next morning all was near forgotten. He always smoothly found a way to distract us after those arguments, whether it was an unexpected hug or playing around. There never was a time you could stay mad at him for long. Besides, I was someone who liked to have drinks with friends once in a while, so I knew what it was like to say the wrong thing and wake up with regrets the next morning.

After dealing with alcoholism, my parents knew this about me and it caused friction in our home. I was strong-willed and they were fighting to correct me knowing the dangers I was facing. I moved out at a young age unable to successfully communicate with them. At the time, it seemed the best choice. Like many young people, I felt I knew everything, and they just weren't getting it. One day years later with a family of my own, I finally get it.

Fast forwarding now to the day my parents were saved. I remember being there and being skeptical and confused. It was completely out of my dad's character for him to do something like that. At that moment, I remember feeling overwhelmed with emotion and wondering what was happening.

I believe my thought process in the days and weeks following that day was something to the extent of, that's great as long as they don't think I'll be going to church every Sunday. Other than that, I never thought much about it.

My curiosity was first peaked about God during one of my mom's heart to hearts with me. I was maturing, growing, and our barriers were falling so we were talking more, but I still wasn't going to church. She said to me that she would pray often that I would be saved and discover a relationship with God. She was frustrated that this prayer wasn't being answered.

She told me her prayer was finally answered one day when God told her He was coming for me. Boom, that hit me like a ton of bricks. He was coming for me. Though God had not answered her prayer the way she expected, she knew she had to leave it in God's capable hands. What she didn't know was that what she told me shook me then and to this day still does.

However, I continued to live my life in the norm with no desire to follow them down their new path. That was until, my husband and I became pregnant with our first child. Excitement and anticipation filled each day leading up to our first ultrasound. I will never forget the silence that fell over that room when the ultrasound tech found something of concern. All of a sudden this God I wanted to only know in theory became the only one I could trust. I wanted to be angry with Him and blame Him. How could I, though, if I wanted Him to deliver me a healthy baby. From that moment, my husband and I prayed daily. Often something like this: "Dear God, we will do anything. We will attend church every Sunday. Prove to us that You exist. Heal our baby. Please God we beg You. In Jesus Name. Amen." We had hope, we had God, and with that everything was going to be okay.

Late June in 2007, our precious daughter was born and then rushed to the NICU due to complications during labor and delivery. In the haze of the anesthetic, I remember two things vividly. One, holding my daughter in my arms, and memorizing every inch of her. Secondly, asking my father to pray for and baptize her. We had roughly twelve hours with her that day before she passed away. I will keep those twelve hours near my heart until the day I hold her again.

Months and years passed, then in another heart to heart with my parents, I shared one of my frustrations.

"How could God take her from me?" I asked.

Their response was, "You need to understand, God did not take her from you, He received her."

Be still my heart! God saved her from the pain of this broken world and is keeping her for me with Him. Without my parents' teachings and guidance since the day they were saved, I would never have learned about God's love for me or His love for those I hold dear. My parents' faith is unwavering. To this day, with three beautiful children, my husband and I know we can go to my parents with any question, for any prayer request, any time of the day or night.

I still do not have the relationship with God that my parents do, however I can honestly say now, I aspire to!

-Laurie Loitz

Amanda shares...

In my eyes, I had a pretty normal upbringing. My Dad worked away lots, but when he was home we always had fun together. Whether it was watching wrestling on TV or wrestling on the living room floor with all us girls piling on top of him, we would have a good time. I would say I was a bit of a tomboy, so I felt a bit like the son my dad never had. I always enjoyed that bond with my dad and loved that we both could make each other laugh because our sense of humor is so much the same.

My mom was always there for us and tried her best to hold down the fort while my dad was away. We loved our mom very much, but once dad was gone to work we would give her a run for her money with our shenanigans. She has such a soft heart that we knew we could sweet talk her into a lesser punishment for our silly behavior than we could our dad.

When mom and dad were both home, we would all have fun going to the lake, camping, watching movies, etc. We went to church on Sundays and all us girls went to classes in order to be confirmed. After being confirmed, we did not go to church as much. Usually just during the holidays and then sometimes not then either. As a kid, I always believed in God and somewhat knew the importance of the commandments, but never really had a relationship with Him.

Growing up in a Lutheran church that was what I would call more reserved, I was always relieved when we didn't have to go to church. I always found it very boring and hard to keep my eyes open, so I never looked forward to going. I can remember the morning my mom came into my bedroom and said we were going to church because my Aunt and Uncle were up from BC and they wanted us to join them at a different church for a service that day. I was annoyed, lying in bed, still tired, and could hear my dad telling her that she didn't have to make us go and that she could go on her own. I thought, *Sweet we don't have to go.* Then my mom came in pouting and giving me this classic guilt trip. I started to feel bad for not wanting to go, so I got up, got ready, and we all ended up going, even dad.

I still remember not believing how upbeat and fun this new church seemed. The music was more contemporary and they had a live band! That just was **not** what I was used to in the Lutheran church, but it was awesome. The pastor even found ways to make jokes while preaching which made it easy to engage and actually pay attention to what he was saying. Although as a teen, I still would have rather been other places, at least it was a more enjoyable experience.

Then, the unthinkable happened. The pastor gave an altar call and of **all** people, **my dad** got up and started heading to the altar. I seriously could not believe my eyes. My dad was the last person that you would think would ever do something like that! In fact, he didn't even want to go to church that morning. I wondered what the heck he was doing going up there. I was so confused, but at the same time so proud of my dad. It actually made me close to tears to see him humbly go up there and be prayed over. To see him so vulnerable, so honest, and so out of his comfort zone was really eye opening.

I can easily say that from that day on everything changed. That day my parents gave their hearts to God made a huge change in their lives. My parents who used to party and drink and fight were now not drinking at all. Instead, they were going to Bible studies and were practically best friends with the pastor and his wife. My mom even became a part of the worship team and would go up on stage and sing during worship service. It was so cool to see my mom break out of her shell.

As a kid, I remember thinking it was great they found God, but wondering why did they have to do it while I was hitting my prime teenage years. These were the years where I wanted to start partying and having a "good" time. My sisters got to have parties and not only that my parents would have drinks with their friends at these parties. Now I figured I wasn't going to get to have the same fun they did. Even though I was worried about that, it in no way hindered my teenage experiences. I still had fun, still went to parties, and still had a good time, but had the love and support from two Christian parents that guided my choices while still allowing me to have fun.

Yes, I still made mistakes along the way, but I was always able to come home to a loving, forgiving, and stable home filled with God's presence. I don't know why, but for some reason I was a little embarrassed about my parents and their new lifestyle. I was always worried they would be called Bible thumpers and never wanted that to happen. Looking back, it's so funny the little things that I thought mattered when in fact they were so trivial.

After they were saved, I would hear my dad talking about his testimony and I could not believe the internal battles he was facing. If my parents hadn't told me, I would never have known my dad was an alcoholic. I knew he had drinks with company and remember seeing him "hung over" on the couch here and there, but really had no idea that he was battling addiction. Even so, it's amazing how God completely delivered him from his addiction. My parents were in such a better place after finding God and they have been so blessed ever since. They overcame addiction, enormous debt, and have built a booming business from the ground up.

It is hard to imagine what all of our lives would be like today if we had not gone into church that Sunday morning. Even though there were times I wished it would have happened after my high school years, now when I look back I realize I am the lucky one who got to have a front row seat in their transformation and as a result I was building a relationship with God and didn't even realize it. Hearing the stories my parents would tell of prayers being answered and listening to the pastor, I found myself praying every night and knowing that God was going to answer them in one way or another.

As years passed and I became more secure with myself, I stopped feeling embarrassed about my parents' relationship with God and became proud of that relationship and wanted to know more. It was so nice to be able to ask my parents the questions I had about God, Jesus, and the Bible. They were always there to give me guidance and taught me how important it was to have a relationship with God. I truly believe it is the reason I have the relationship with God that I do today. My husband and I are now both on our own journey of building our relationship with Him and showing our kids the importance of that just as my parents did me.

-Amanda Priddle

Digging Deeper

As you read these stories from our daughters, do you see the importance of the legacy you are creating for your children and your children's children?

What does Proverbs 13:22 have to say about this?

Do you believe there is a generational curse like alcoholism or some other form of addiction coming against your family?

We hold on to these promises for our children that they too will serve the Lord. It may or not be in our lifetime, but it will be.

And if it seems evil to you to serve the Lord, choose for yourselves this day whom you will serve, whether the gods which your fathers served that were on the other side of the River, or the gods of the Amorites, in whose land you dwell. But as for me and my house, we will serve the Lord." (Joshua 24:15)

Just as there can be generational curses there can also be generational blessings. If you and your house serve the Lord, you can pass that on to the next generation.

Therefore know that the Lord your God, He is God, the faithful God who keeps covenant and mercy for a thousand generations with those who love Him and keep His commandments. (Deuteronomy 7:9)

Pray and ask the Lord to reveal any generational curses that have come against your children or your children's children. Seek other prayer warriors and pray together to break all strongholds against you and your family in the name of Jesus. Thank God for His generational blessings on your family as well.

CONCLUSION

Walking with the Lord

We have continued walking with the Lord and enjoying the lessons He has been teaching us. We sold our acreage and moved into town to help defray our living expenses. One day I told Aurelie I had a job interview in Edmonton, but I felt that for some reason God didn't want me to have that job. We just walked in that trust and when God said yes, we did it and when God said no we did not. When He told me not to take that job, I went through the interview, but told them I couldn't accept the job. One thing we have learned is that His way is always the best way.

One day, God sat me down at the foot of the bed as Aurelie was getting ready for work. He told me He didn't want me reading those little daily messages of hope written by someone else anymore. When I asked Him why, He said I was using them like a horoscope. When He said that I realized every time I read the daily message, I would take that little message and use it to set my mindset for the day. God wanted to show me through His Word and our time together how to set my mindset for the day. So I quit reading it and now I only read the Bible. As I did that every morning, I would pray and seek His face for that day. It was amazing the walk that we walked and the trust that we had as we stayed totally focused on Him.

Anytime God asks us to give, we try very hard to be obedient. He has never steered us wrong and we have no reason to doubt Him. I'll tell you we've never wanted for anything. God has looked after our every need and looked after our finances. The enemy still tries to get in there and tries to convince us God isn't there for us. However, he has never won out because God has always been there for us. Through all the good times and through the really bad times, God has shown us we can count on Him.

We have three wonderful daughters, two wonderful son in-laws, and eight amazing grandchildren. We love spending time with our family. It's just incredible the blessings God has given us in so many wonderful ways.

We did have a little set back when the church we were going to fell apart. The congregation attacked the pastor, there was an unfortunate series of events and the church got shut down. It just blew the wind out of our sails for a while. We started looking around trying to find what we were supposed to do, where we should go, and where we belonged. It seemed like we had no answer from God, so we just stopped, rested, and just had home church.

However, after a while we started to slip away. We didn't fellowship with other Christians much anymore. It was just easier to stay at home, have coffee, and watch the preacher on TV. We began to notice little things slipping away, we started allowing things to happen, we started being okay with things a little more than we should be, and we were not accountable to anybody. One day, we decided it was time to see if God was going to send us to a new church family.

We began to go to church with our daughter, son-in-law, and their family. We got plugged in again and it has been awesome. Now we are attending our home church and going to a Bible study as well. We will just see what God wants from us on this new path He has chosen for us. We know He asked that we write this book, so we have been diligently working to complete our assignment. Aurelie and I both have a heart for some kind of ministry, we just don't know yet what it is. We do know that God will direct us. Whatever it is, if it's from God, it will be well worth the wait.

At first, we used to be scared of God and the power He has, but we have come to know Him and love that we are able to come boldly and humbly to the throne room and spend time with Him. It is amazing that someday every knee shall bow, and every tongue confess what an amazing God we serve.

Diligently Study the Word of God

When we are diligent in our reading of the Bible, that is when His Word is a lamp to our feet. We really don't understand why we don't read it more often because of the direction it points us. We know we would be more capable in dealing with what this world has to offer if we did spend more time studying and meditating on His Word. So many times His Word has set us on a course so different from what we were used to living and what a glorious path it has been! Our prayer is that we will be more consistent, and daily turn to His Word for direction for our lives.

Your word is a lamp to my feet and a light to my path.
(Psalm 119:105)

For example, I had been offered a position at work. It was an exciting but scary position. I was sure when I went to sleep that I was going to accept the job. Then I woke up with so much anxiety about taking the job that I wanted to tell them that they had offered the wrong person the job and that they should give it to someone else. The day before I had just signed up for Bible Gateway's verse of the day and that morning Isaiah 48:17 was my very first verse. After reading this verse, I accepted the position and trusted that God was in control. We have learned to give God complete control of our lives. We pray for direction when making decisions and we have learned to trust and go in the way God has told us to.

> *Thus says the LORD, your Redeemer, the Holy One of Israel: "I am the LORD your God, Who teaches you to profit, Who leads you by the way you should go." (Isaiah 48:17)*

There have been so many times in our life when we wanted to do things our way, but knew it was not the right way. So, we opted to take the straight and narrow. In the end our own selfish desires were unimportant and would have gained us nothing of true value. We have turned to the scriptures when tempted to do something we know is wrong.

> *You are of God, little children, and have overcome them, because He who is in you is greater than he who is in the world. (1 John 4:4)*

So many times we have been worried about certain things, such as money to pay bills but God is always faithful to meet our needs.

> *Trust in the LORD with all your heart, and lean not on your own understanding; In all your ways acknowledge Him, and He shall direct your paths. (Proverbs 3:5-6)*

There was sin in my life that I had to confess to my husband and for days I struggled with telling him. I was scared he would leave me the moment he found out. He was angry, but it did not change his love for me. He forgave me and we grew closer together. It was not easy for him, but it was possible through Christ who strengthens us.

I can do all things through Christ who strengthens me. (Philippians 4:13)

When it was time for me to tell my husband about the sins that the enemy was constantly raking me over the coals for, 1 John 1:9 became very true. When I told Shannon everything I had done, he forgave me and the constant thoughts and worries went away. It is a very important step in forgiveness to confess it. It helps break the stronghold of the enemy

If we confess our sins, He is faithful and just to forgive us our sins and to cleanse us from all unrighteousness. (1 John 1:9)

When we first accepted Jesus, we could never think that Jesus would accept us just as we were. We had done so much wrong in our life. How could someone so perfect accept us? Romans 8:1 and 2 Corinthians 5:17 became the foundation of our faith. It brings us great comfort to know that we are not trapped in our sin.

Therefore, if anyone is in Christ, he is a new creation; old things have passed away; behold, all things have become new. (2 Corinthians 5:17)

There is therefore now no condemnation to those who are in Christ Jesus, who do not walk according to the flesh, but according to the Spirit. (Romans 8:1)

When we became Christians, we started looking for ways to earn our way into heaven. Then when we would do something wrong, the enemy was very quick to tell us we had undone anything good we may have accomplished and that our salvation was gone. This was such a heavy burden we were trying to bear. Then we read Ephesians 2:8 and our Creator spoke to our hearts. Salvation was a gift and it was given to us. We couldn't work for it and we did nothing to earn it, nor could we. If we couldn't earn it then we couldn't lose it, either. Just as we give our children gifts, our Father gave us the gift of salvation through His Son Jesus Christ.

For by grace you have been saved through faith, and that not of yourselves; it is the gift of God. (Ephesians 2:8)

Before we gave our lives to Christ, I recall going to bed at night and when I closed my eyes I would see dark shadows hovering over me. When I gave my heart to the Lord that darkness disappeared. Not only that, it wasn't me choosing Him, it was Him calling me.

But you are a chosen generation, a royal priesthood, a holy nation, His own special people, that you may proclaim the praises of Him who called you out of darkness into His marvelous light. (1 Peter 2:9)

I have struggled with being overweight my entire life. I went to a Christian conference and one of the speakers there referred to Proverbs

23:7. She wasn't speaking about weight at the time, but it rang true for me and my weight. As long as I kept thinking about how overweight I was, I was making my body what my mind thought. I immediately began a diet and exercise regime, and over the course of time I lost 100 pounds. Now I would love to say I am at my goal weight, but just like my faith it is a work in progress. Whenever I feel sick or scared I revert to this scripture

> *For as he thinks in his heart, so is he. "Eat and drink!" he says to you, but his heart is not with you.* (Proverbs 23:7)

Over the course of our walk, we have learned that God wants justice, but He wants mercy from us in order to get it. It is important to remember this as we are often very quick to judge others. God doesn't need us to judge anyone, for it is by that standard we too will be judged. We learned very quickly that it is only by the grace of God that we are who we are, but for by the grace of God there go I. It is because of God's mercy that we are able to walk from the darkness into the light.

> *He has shown you, O man, what is good; and what does the* LORD *require of you but to do justly, to love mercy, and to walk humbly with your God.* (Micah 6:8)

Recently, I went through a very difficult situation at a job I had been at over sixteen years. I began waking up crying every night at 3 a.m. with so much anxiety I couldn't go back to sleep. A friend reminded me the Father loved me so much that He held all my tears in a bottle. Knowing the Father kept my tears in a bottle really helped me to understand how much He loved and cared about me. It is awesome to know that when life gets us down God is there to comfort us.

You number my wanderings; put my tears into Your bottle; are they not in Your book. (Psalm 56:8)

So many times we worry about things or want things, but the bottom line is God knows exactly what we need and exactly when we need it. Many times we thought we really needed something only in time to learn that we really didn't need it, we just wanted it. Since giving our lives to Christ, there are no **needs** in our life. They are all fulfilled. God has proven to be faithful in this…every time.

"Therefore do not worry, saying, 'What shall we eat?' or 'What shall we drink?' or 'What shall we wear?' For after all these things the Gentiles seek. For your heavenly Father knows that you need all these things. But seek first the kingdom of God and His righteousness, and all these things shall be added to you. Therefore do not worry about tomorrow, for tomorrow will worry about its own things. Sufficient for the day is its own trouble. (Matthew 6:31-34)

We learned that if you follow Psalm 37:4, He loves us so much He will give us the desires of our hearts. It may not look like we thought it would, though. The reason we say that is because sometimes He changes the desires of your heart.

Delight yourself also in the Lord, And He shall give you the desires of your heart. (Psalm 37:4)

This scripture was my very first memory verse! I just loved the fact that as soon as I die I get to be in Heaven. I don't have to sleep for years in a dark hole in the ground. I get to walk on streets of gold with Jesus! This brings us great comfort whenever the thought of dying comes to mind.

Jesus said to him, "Assuredly, I say to you, today you will be with Me in Paradise." (Luke 23:43)

On my way to work one day in March, I rolled my vehicle. It had rained the night before and there was a lot of black ice. I was going 100km an hour when my SUV went sideways. I knew in an instant I was in a lot of trouble. I just called out for Jesus to please save me. In that moment, I thought I might actually die. There was no fear though as all I wanted to do was be present with my Savior. My work here was not yet done and I give glory to God for surviving that accident so I can finish my assignment.

Call upon Me in the day of trouble; I will deliver you, and you shall glorify Me. (Psalm 50:15)

There are times in our selfishness that we have gone astray wanting something worldly, but we have always been able to run back to the cross for forgiveness and mercy. This scripture is heart breaking. It breaks our heart to read that our iniquity was laid on Jesus Christ on the cross, but yet at the same time it showed us how very much He loved us.

All we like sheep have gone astray; we have turned, every one, to his own way; and the LORD has laid on Him the iniquity of us all. (Isaiah 53:6)

There are so many times that we wanted to turn away from our sin. We would try and try and fail almost every time. We couldn't figure out why we couldn't stop doing what we did not want to do, after all we were Christians now so we figured it should be easy to walk away. Then we read Romans 7:17-20 and it was so freeing! Finally, someone in the Bible related to us. He had the same struggles as us and helped us to see why we did what we did. God removed our sin as far as the east is from the west and we know that it is not in our own strength that we can resist temptation.

> *But now, it is no longer I who do it, but sin that dwells in me. For I know that in me (that is, in my flesh) nothing good dwells; for to will is present with me, but how to perform what is good I do not find. For the good that I will to do, I do not do; but the evil I will not to do, that I practice. Now if I do what I will not to do, it is no longer I who do it, but sin that dwells in me.* (Romans 7:17-20)

When we lost our granddaughter, the Lord had to be near each and every one of us in order for us to get through that day and the days that followed. There has been no pain like the pain we experienced that day. I honestly questioned if there was a God. Thankfully, He stayed near. When we are weak He is strong.

> *The LORD is near to those who have a broken heart, and saves such as have a contrite spirit.* (Psalm 34:18)

No matter what we are going through, time and time again 1 Peter 5:7 would come through our minds. We would lean very heavy on this scripture, especially when things were so very bad we don't know where else to turn. It is so important to cast our cares on Him immediately so we do not become so overburdened. We have learned this lesson the hard way.

Casting all your care upon Him, for He cares for you. (1 Peter 5:7)

John 14:13 has had both positive and negative effects in my life. I depended greatly on this scripture when everything was going wrong with our granddaughter. I didn't get the results I wanted, so I thought it couldn't be true. Then I have seen other prayers come to full fruition. I don't understand the how or why, I have just learned to trust the Father's heart.

And whatever you ask in My name, that I will do, that the Father may be glorified in the Son. (John 14:13)

I always have to remember that no matter what is going on, Jeremiah 29:11 is God's word to me and I must trust and walk in it. Despite what is going on in this world, it is mind blowing to know what an awesome and loving God we serve.

For I know the thoughts that I think toward you, says the L*ORD*, *thoughts of peace and not of evil, to give you a future and a hope.* (Jeremiah 29:11)

When I need a check point of what faith should look like, Hebrews 11:1 tells me what I need to know. The best times and walks in our lives are when we totally rely on God in faith.

Now faith is the substance of things hoped for, the evidence of things not seen. (Hebrews 11:1)

1 Kings 3:5 was instrumental in Shannon's health. God woke me up and told me to read my Bible and when I did, I was reading about Solomon.

At Gibeon the LORD appeared to Solomon in a dream by night; and God said, "Ask! What shall I give you? (1 Kings 3:5)

Matthew 11:28 is a verse we should have tattooed across our foreheads! So many times I try and fix things in my own strength and then I spend so much time upset and sick to my stomach thinking about the situations I shouldn't even be involved in. When I finally have had enough, then I turn to the Father and collapse in His arms that were waiting there right from the beginning.

Come to Me, all you who labor and are heavy laden, and I will give you rest. (Matthew 11:28)

We love Lamentations 3:22-23. His mercies are new **every morning**! Now we can live freely knowing even when we do give into sin that God's mercy is new every morning. Praise the Lord! Every morning, we can come to the cross and ask for forgiveness and strength to make it through another day.

Through the LORD's mercies we are not consumed, because His compassions fail not. They are new every morning; great is Your faithfulness. (Lamentations 3:22-23)

We hold on to these promises for our children that they too will serve the Lord. It may or not be in our lifetime, but it will be.

> *And if it seems evil to you to serve the Lord, choose for yourselves this day whom you will serve, whether the gods which your fathers served that were on the other side of the River, or the gods of the Amorites, in whose land you dwell. But as for me and my house, we will serve the Lord."* (Joshua 24:15)

Just as there can be generational curses there can also be generational blessings. If you and your house serve the Lord, you can pass that on to the next generation.

> *Therefore know that the Lord your God, He is God, the faithful God who keeps covenant and mercy for a thousand generations with those who love Him and keep His commandments.* (Deuteronomy 7:9)

We would walk by other people's places and wish we could have their house, car or boat, but when we gave our hearts to God, we found out that stuff like that does not matter anymore. We have learned that if we walk in His ways, we will be content. He truly does know what we need.

> *Let your conduct be without covetousness; be content with such things as you have. For He Himself has said, "I will never leave you nor forsake you."* (Hebrews 13:5)

Sometimes you can't help but wonder why certain events are happening. We often feel that if we are Christians we should not be facing such trials and tribulations. We ask, "Why is this happening to me? This isn't what was prayed for? What is going on? Why is God allowing this?" When faced with those moments, we must trust in God's Word and the promise of verses like John 16:33.

> *"I have told you these things so you may have peace in Me. In the world you will have much trouble. But take hope! I have power over the world!"* (John 16:33)

God is always in control no matter what circumstance you are facing. Trust in Him.

> *And we know that all things work together for good to those who love God, to those who are the called according to His purpose.* (Romans 8:28)

Thank You so much, Father God that Your Son, Jesus Christ died for our sins so we can walk in His righteousness.

> *For God so loved the world that He gave His only begotten Son, that whoever believes in Him should not perish but have everlasting life.* (John 3:16)

We all need to be His disciples. The best way to do that is to show Christ's work in our lives. We need to live a life that shows others how much we believe in and trust God. What we do and how we face challenges often speak louder than our words.

Conclusion

Then He said to them, "Follow Me, and I will make you fishers of men." (Matthew 4:19)

Every time we walk through troubled times we read and quoted scripture. We know God's Word has power to move our mountains so we speak His Word and are not ashamed of the gospel.

For I am not ashamed of the gospel of Christ, for it is the power of God to salvation for everyone who believes, for the Jew first and also for the Greek. For in it the righteousness of God is revealed from faith to faith; as it is written, "The just shall live by faith." (Romans 1:16-17)

Our goal as His disciples is to continue to die to ourselves and our selfish desires, and walk closer with God and let Him consume us.

He must increase, but I must decrease. (John 3:30)

Therefore God also has highly exalted Him and given Him the name which is above every name, that at the name of Jesus every knee should bow, of those in heaven, and of those on earth, and of those under the earth, and that every tongue should confess that Jesus Christ is Lord, to the glory of God the Father. (Philippians 2:9-11)

We love You Father God!
Seek justice, love mercy, and walk humbly with your God.

For More Information
Contact Shannon and Aurelie through:

sareeve@outlook.com